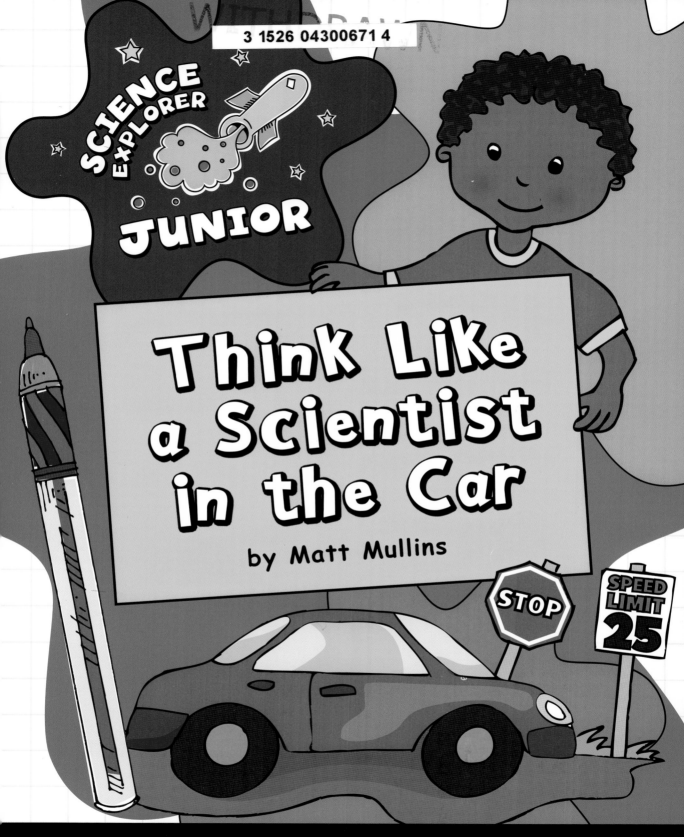

SCIENCE EXPLORER JUNIOR

Think Like a Scientist in the Car

by Matt Mullins

STOP

SPEED LIMIT 25

CHERRY LAKE PUBLISHING · ANN ARBOR, MICHIGAN

Published in the United States of America by Cherry Lake Publishing
Ann Arbor, Michigan
www.cherrylakepublishing.com

Content Editor: Robert Wolffe, EdD, Professor of Teacher Education,
Bradley University, Peoria, Illinois

Design and Illustration: The Design Lab

Photo Credits: Page 8, ©Dmitriy Shironosov/Shutterstock, Inc.; page
11, ©Elena Elisseeva/Shutterstock, Inc.; page 12, ©INTERFOTO/
Alamy; page 17, ©Adrian Britton/Shutterstock, Inc.; pages 18 and 25,
©Media Bakery; page 19, ©timy/Shutterstock, Inc.; page 20, ©Yellowj/
Shutterstock, Inc.; page 21, ©Pics-xl/Shutterstock, Inc.; page 28, ©Lisa F.
Young/Shutterstock, Inc.

Library of Congress Cataloging-in-Publication Data
Mullins, Matt.
  Think like a scientist in the car/by Matt Mullins.
      p. cm.—(Science explorer junior)
  Includes bibliographical references and index.
  ISBN-13: 978-1-61080-164-5 (lib. bdg.)
  ISBN-10: 1-61080-164-4 (lib. bdg.)
  1. Automobiles—Juvenile literature. 2. Science—Methodology—Juvenile
literature. I. Title.
  TL147.M854 2012
  629.222—dc22   2011007046

Cherry Lake Publishing would like to acknowledge the work
of The Partnership for 21st Century Skills. Please visit
www.21stcenturyskills.org for more information.

Printed in the United States of America
Corporate Graphics Inc.
July 2011
CLFA09

TABLE OF CONTENTS

How Does That Work?

Car engines are made up of many different parts.

Have you ever looked at something and wondered, "How does that work?" Scientists do that all the time. Even in a car.

Even pets like riding in cars.

Cars are wonderful. They get us to school, to grandmother's house, and home. You can learn a lot about science in a car. How far can it be driven? How does **motion** work? When you're in the car, why do things look like they go by so fast? Scientists asking these questions study **physics**. You can study physics in the car!

STEP-BY-STEP

You can get your own answers by thinking like a scientist. Go step by step. You may have to repeat some steps as you go.

1. Observe what is going on.
2. Ask a question.
3. Guess the answer. This is called a **hypothesis**.
4. Design an **experiment** to test your idea.
5. Gather materials to test your idea.
6. Write down what happens.
7. Make a **conclusion**.

Don't forget your note pad!

Use words and numbers to write down what you've learned. It's okay if the experiment doesn't work. Try changing something, and then do the experiment again.

Always write down your observations.

GET THE FACTS

Teachers and librarians can help you find information.

Scientists look for facts before they start an experiment. They use this information as a place to start.

Where can you find information? A library is filled with books, magazines, and science videos that can help you. Your parents may have books.

You can talk to a teacher or a parent. You can visit a museum, too.

You can also find facts on the Internet. Be careful. Not everything on the Internet is the truth. Ask an adult to help you find the best places to look for information.

Be careful anytime you go online.

How Far Can It Go?

Have you ever noticed the dials on a car's dashboard?

Have you ever seen a car commercial on television? Sometimes you will hear about a car's "MPG" rating. This refers to "miles per gallon," which is how far it can be driven on a gallon of gasoline. The higher the MPG, the more driving you can get out of a gallon of gas.

What kind of car does your family have?

Cars are very heavy. Moving them requires a lot of energy. Cars have engines that run on energy made from gasoline. The engines turn a shaft connected to the wheels. This moves the car.

A scientist named Rudolf Diesel had an idea. He thought the engines used in cars did not work very well. He thought that they wasted fuel. Diesel wanted a more efficient engine. He worked with an engine like the one used by Karl Benz. Benz had invented the first car powered by gasoline.

Karl Benz paved the way for modern cars.

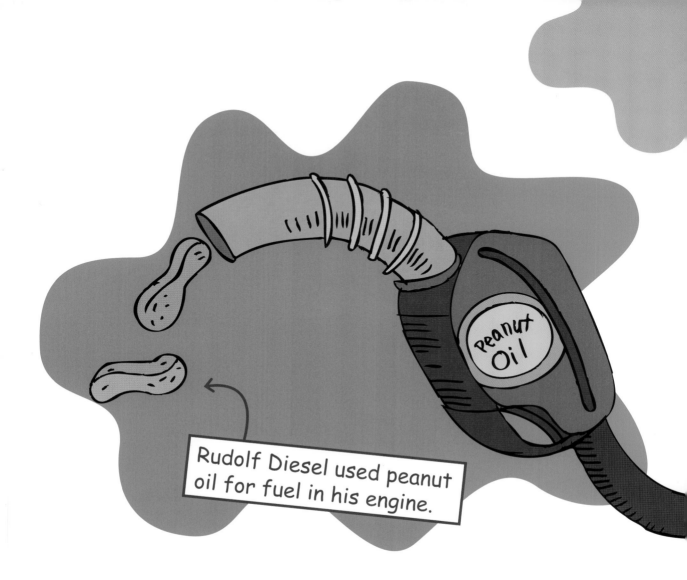

Rudolf Diesel used peanut oil for fuel in his engine.

Diesel redesigned the engine. In his engine, he put the air inside under higher pressure than in other **combustion** engines. This compressed air got hot. Then the engine sprayed in fuel, and the hot air blew it up. The explosion moved the **driveshaft** and wheels. Diesel named his engine after himself.

DO AN EXPERIMENT

Miles:
43,291

Take careful notes.

You can measure how many miles per gallon (or miles per liter) your car gets. Wait for the next time your parents fill your family car's gas tank. That is when you will begin doing your science. Ask your parents how many miles are on the car. Write that down. Ask them to be sure to take you with them the next time they fill the gas tank.

The next time your parents fill the gas tank, write down how many miles are on the car. Subtract the first number of miles you wrote down from this number. That is how many miles you traveled between fill-ups. Now ask your parents how many gallons of gas were put into the tank. Divide the number of miles traveled by the number of gallons added. Your answer is your miles per gallon!

Mileage at fill-up: 43,867
Beginning mileage: −43,291
Miles traveled: 576

Number of gallons of
gas put into the tank: 18

$576 \div 18 = 32$ MPG

Always double check your math.

Move It!

It is important to avoid wasting gas.

34 MILES

17 MILES

Why do you think miles per gallon is important? Let's say your car only gets 17 miles per gallon. This means every gallon of gas gets you 17 miles toward wherever you are going. Maybe your car gets 34 miles per gallon, instead. That means you can drive twice as far on one gallon of gas!

Cars get different MPG ratings based on where they drive. Most cars get lower MPG driving in the city than on the highway. Why do you think that is? What happens a lot in the city that doesn't happen on the highway?

There are a lot of stop signs in towns and cities.

A scientist named Isaac Newton studied physics a long time ago. Newton developed important ideas about motion. The first one simply explains that objects tend to keep doing what they're doing. If a car is going along at a certain speed, it will keep going at that speed. If it is stopped, it will stay stopped unless a force acts on it.

Isaac Newton discovered many important rules about the way our world works.

Drivers must always keep an eye on their speed.

For drivers, this means that it can be best to reach a certain speed and then stick to it. The less you put on the brakes or increase the speed, the better. Engines run most efficiently without interruption.

DO AN EXPERIMENT

Cars can go very fast on highways.

Can you tell how well your car runs in the city versus on the highway? One way is pretty simple. Just check your MPG on several trips. Compare the results from four or five trips that you and your family take.

Is the MPG higher on trips that are mostly on the highway or on ones in the city? Why do you think it's different? Do you think it matters what time of year you travel? Why or why not?

Cars must drive slower on icy roads.

Watch It!

What do you see outside the car window?

One of the fields of science you can study from your car is **optics**. Look out the car windows as your parents drive. See how fast things near the car go by. Look in the distance at a faraway building or hill or mountain. These barely seem to move at all!

Now look at the speedometer of your car. Does it have a needle that moves over numbers? The numbers indicate how fast the car is going. From straight over the driver's shoulder, the needle looks like it is over one number. From the other side of the car, it looks like it is over a different one.

Only the driver can see exactly where the needle is pointing.

Both of those examples refer to something with a very fancy name: **parallax**. Parallax is the difference in where objects appear to be because of the way they line up differently in your vision.

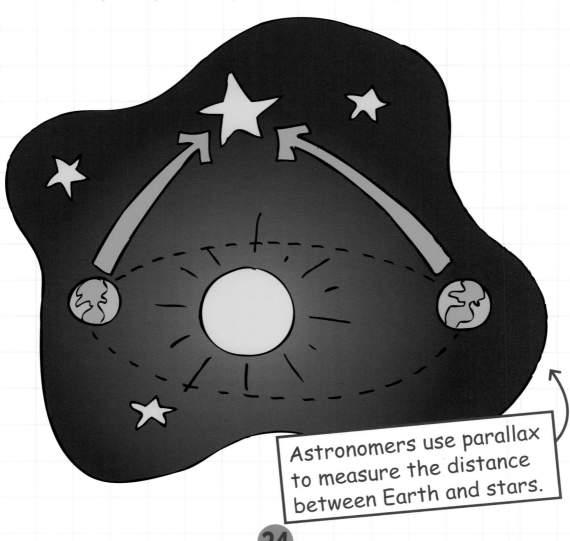

Astronomers use parallax to measure the distance between Earth and stars.

Johannes Kepler

Scientists have studied this and other parts of the field of optics. Johannes Kepler studied parallax so he could better study where stars were in the sky.

DO AN EXPERIMENT

Pay attention to the way objects look as they get closer.

One of the cool things people can see is depth. We can tell when something is far away and when it is close. We can see that something is moving toward us quickly or slowly. We do this because we have two eyes. Our vision is aimed at one thing, but our eyes are in different spots.

You can test your depth perception in the car. Watch the land move by on one side of the car. Notice things that are far and things that are close. Now look away for 2 minutes. Then cover one eye with your hand so it can't see anything. Look out again. Can you tell what is far and what is close? Try covering the other eye. Did you get the same results?

What happens when you cover an eye?

Your Big Idea— Listen!

What else would you like to learn about cars?

With only one eye, we can't see as much depth. Everything is flat, like in a picture. We can see height and width. With our second eye, we can see more depth! You don't experience parallax motion when using only one eye.

What other experiments can you do while driving in your car? What about experimenting with sound? Sound works by moving the air it travels through. Have you noticed that when an ambulance races by, its siren gets higher and sharper as the ambulance gets closer? How does the sound change when it goes by? Who can you ask to explain this? Do you have a hypothesis? You can come up with one in the car!

What will your next car experiment be?

GLOSSARY

combustion (kuhm-BUS-chuhn) burning fuel

conclusion (kuhn-KLOO-zhuhn) the answer or result of an experiment

driveshaft (DRIVE-shaft) a part of an engine that helps send mechanical power to other parts

experiment (ik-SPER-uh-ment) a test of your idea

gas (GAS) short for gasoline, a liquid burned for energy

hypothesis (hye-PAH-thi-sis) a guess

motion (MOH-shuhn) the act of moving

MPG (EM PEE JEE) miles per gallon

optics (OP-tiks) the study of light and the way it moves

parallax (PAR-uh-laks) the difference in where something appears to be from different views

physics (FIZ-iks) the science of matter and energy

FOR MORE INFORMATION

BOOKS

Becker, Helaine. *Science on the Loose: Amazing Activities and Science Facts You'll Never Believe*. Toronto: Maple Tree Press, 2008.

Gianopoulos, Andrea. *Isaac Newton and the Laws of Motion*. Mankato, MN: Capstone Press, 2007.

WEB SITES

Newton's Laws of Motion
teachertech.rice.edu/Participants/louviere/Newton/
Read more about Newton's laws of motion and do some more experiments.

PBS Kids: ZoomSci
pbskids.org/zoom/activities/sci/
Discover activities that will help you learn more about motion and other science topics.

Physics 4 Kids: Mechanics and Motion
www.physics4kids.com/files/motion_intro.html
Read explanations of mechanics and motion.

INDEX

ABOUT THE AUTHOR

Matt Mullins holds a master's degree in the history of science. Matt lives in Madison, Wisconsin, with his son. Formerly a journalist, Matt writes about science, technology, and other topics, and writes and directs short films.